My Master Loves Me

Rebecca Christenson

Kayto & Co. Publishing

Minneapolis | Minnesota | USA

My Master Loves Me

Rebecca Christenson

Kayto & Co. Publishing

Minneapolis | Minnesota | USA

My Master Loves Me

8860 154th Street West
Prior Lake, MN 55372, USA

ISBN-13: 978-1-7375276-0-2

Library of Congress Control Number: 2021913744

Kayto & Co. Publishing
Minneapolis, Minnesota, USA

This Book Belongs To:

❀ 🐾 🐾 🐾 🐾 🐾 🐾 🐾 🐾 🐾 🐾 🐾 🐾 🐾 🐾 ❀

Hanging Out

Dedicated to my grandchildren:

Ellie, Christopher, Max, River, Jack,

and those to come

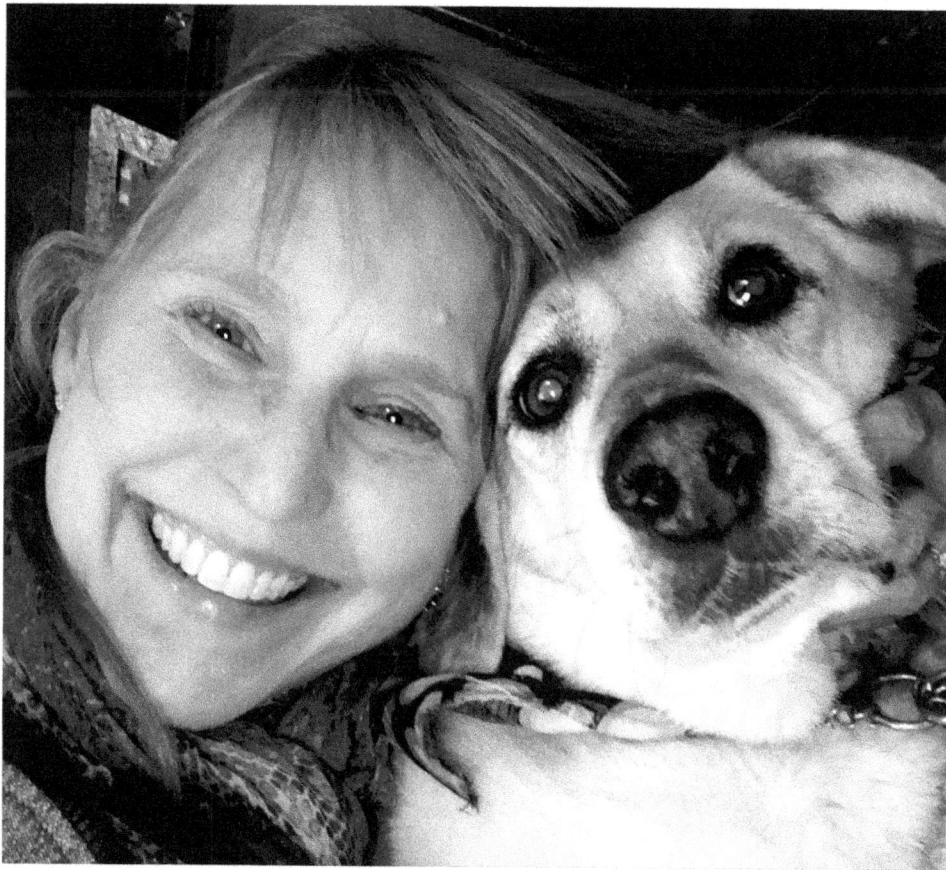

My Master & Me

My master named me Polyester because she thought it was a clever name, but I am a dog of little brain. My master loves me even though I am simple.

I am a mutt. I have purebred friends with fancy fur and collars. My master loves me even though I am a mixed breed.

I am also chubby. The veterinarian tells my master that I need to lose weight, but I like to eat too much. My master loves me even though I am chubby.

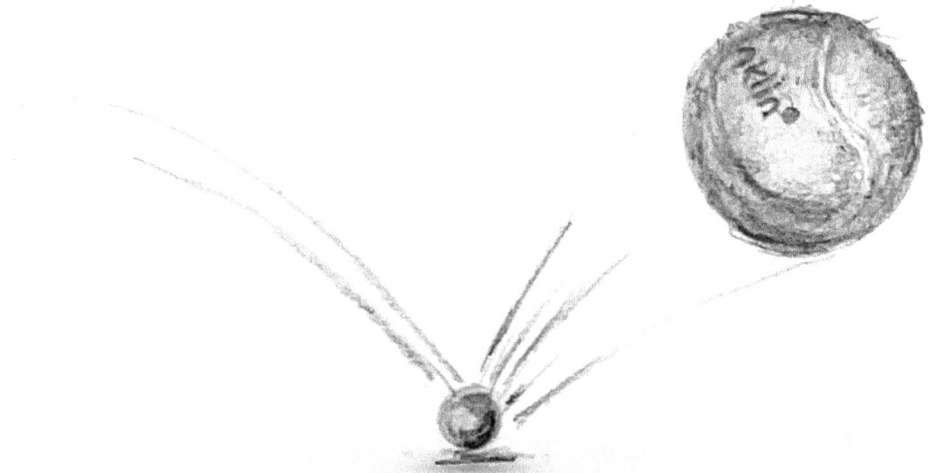

I bark when I shouldn't. When company comes knocking or I see another dog, I just can't help myself. My master loves me even when I bark.

I am naughty. Sometimes when my master leaves, I get bored and lonely and eat the trash.

I leave a big mess. My master scolds me, but she loves me even when I am naughty.

R Christenson

I have accidents sometimes. I have peed on the floor, and I puke after eating the trash. Once or twice I might have pooped in the basement, too. But even when I pee and puke and poop, my master still loves me.

R. Christenson

I am messy. I shed on the floor and furniture. I cause lots of vacuuming and cleaning. I like to roll in smelly stuff and then my master has to give me a bath.

My master loves me even when I shed and stink.

R Cjristenson

I pull and tug on walks. I yank her because I like to smell stuff. Even though I try to go the wrong way, my master still loves me and walks with me.

I cost a lot of money. I have to eat special dog food and expensive medicines. My master takes me to the veterinarian when I am sick and when I need my shots. Even though I cost a lot, my master loves me and thinks I am worth it.

R Christenson

My master has a Master who loves her even if she is simple and chubby and loud and naughty and messy and disobedient. She cost Him a lot, too.

He gave His life for her.

I love my master.

Do you love yours?

R. Cyristenson

The End.

AUTHOR'S NOTE

The inspiration for this book came after a long day when I arrived home to find my entire kitchen floor covered in garbage. A guilty Polyester greeted me. Her remorseful eyes and contrite ears made my anger dissolve.

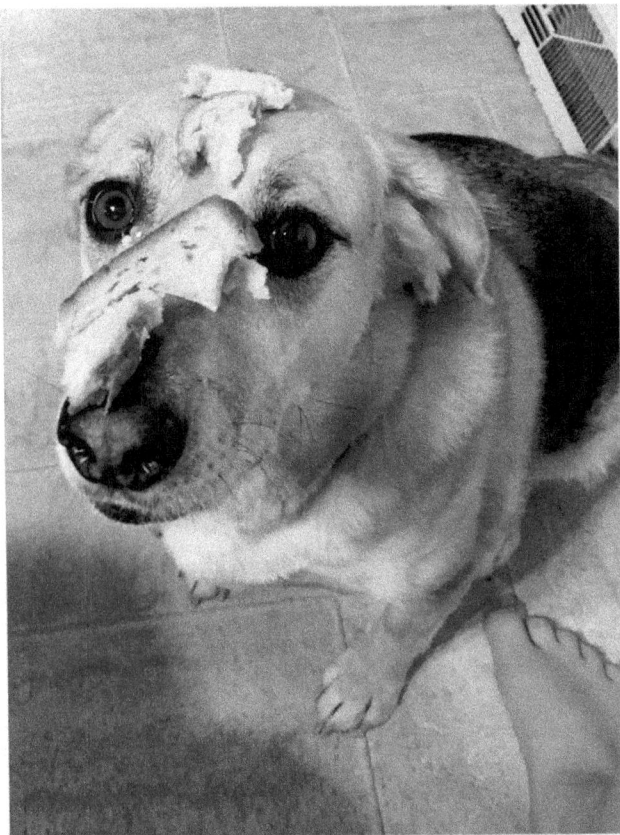

I wondered why I loved this troublesome dog so very much. It struck me that God loves me even though I am even naughtier and more culpable than a dog getting into the trash.

When I was eight years old, my Sunday School teacher told me that God loved me. Showing me a picture of Jesus knocking at a door in a garden, she explained that Jesus was knocking on the door of my heart. She told me that Jesus was too polite to force His way in, but if I wanted to, I could invite Him in. I prayed and asked Him to come in. Even though I was and am not worthy of His extravagant love, He loves me. Even when I neglect Him and disobey Him, His love for me never fails. My love for Polyester, even though it is an imperfect example, reminds me of God's love for me.

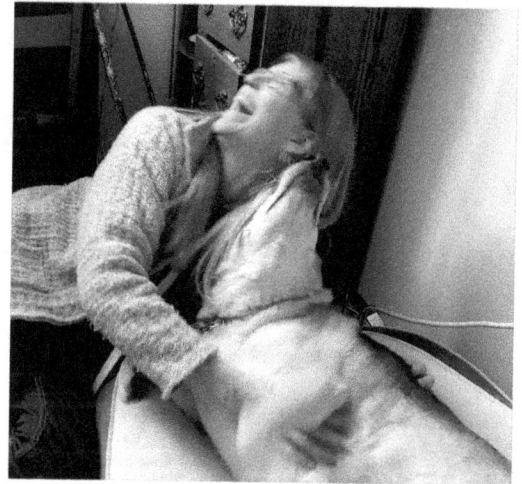

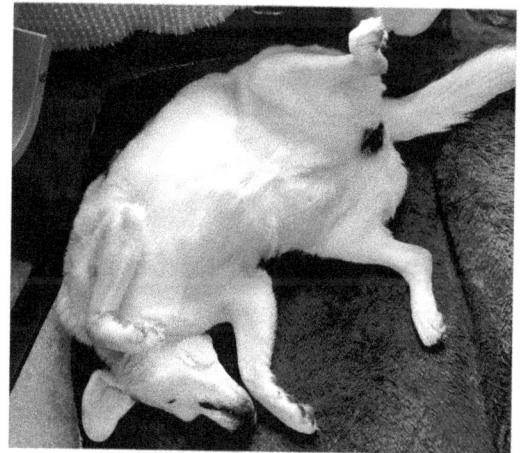

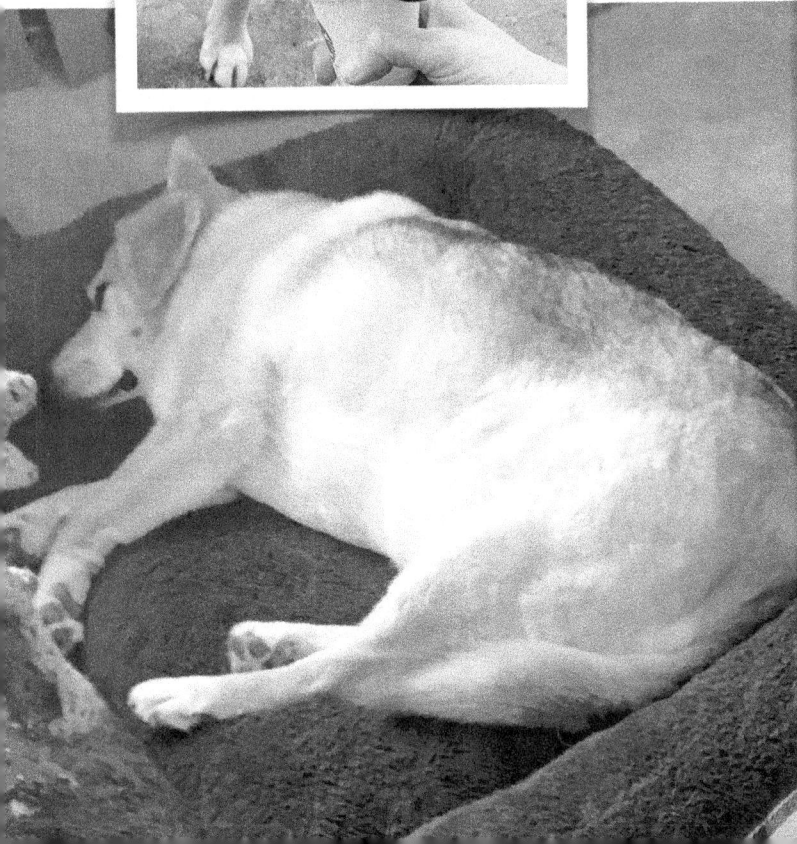

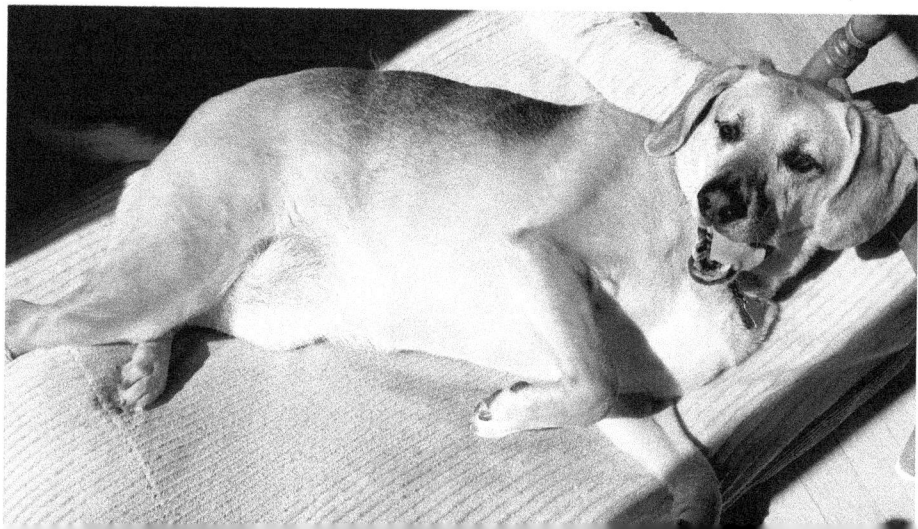

www.ingramcontent.com/pod-product-compliance
Lightning Source LLC
Chambersburg PA
CBHW081252040426
42452CB00015B/2797